PERFECT
PAPER
MOSAICS

PERFECT PAPER MOSAICS

Susan Seymour

Sterling Publishing Co., Inc. New York
A Sterling/Chapelle Book

If you have questions or comments, please contact:
Chapelle, Ltd., Inc.,
P.O. Box 9252, Ogden, UT 84409
(801) 621-2777 • (801) 621-2788 Fax
e-mail: chapelle@chapelleltd.com
web site: chapelleltd.com

Photography: Ryne Hazen, Hazen Imaging

The copy, photographs, instructions, illustrations, and designs in this volume are intended for the personal use of the reader and may be reproduced for that purpose only. Any other use, especially commercial use, is forbidden under law without the written permission of the copyright holder.

Every effort has been made to ensure that all information in this book is accurate. However, due to differing conditions, tools, and individual skills, the publisher cannot be responsible for any injuries, losses, and/or other damages which may result from the use of the information in this book.

This volume is meant to stimulate craft ideas. If readers are unfamiliar or not proficient in a skill necessary to attempt a project, we urge that they refer to an instructional book specifically addressing the required technique.

Library of Congress Cataloging-in-Publication Data available

Seymour, Susan.
  Perfect paper mosaics / Susan Seymour.
     p. cm.
"A Sterling/Chapelle Book."
Includes index.
  ISBN 1-4027-1656-7
1. Mosaics--Technique. 2. Paper work. I. Title.

TT910.S4 2005
738.5'6--dc22

                                                        2005001056

10 9 8 7 6 5 4 3 2 1
Published by Sterling Publishing Co., Inc.
387 Park Avenue South, New York, NY 10016
©2005 by Susan Seymour
Distributed in Canada by Sterling Publishing
c/o Canadian Manda Group, 165 Dufferin Street
Toronto, Ontario, Canada M6K 3H6
Distributed in Great Britain by Chrysalis Books Group PLC,
The Chrysalis Building Bramley Road, London W10 6SP, England
Distributed in Australia by Capricorn Link (Australia) Pty. Ltd.
P. O. Box 704, Windsor, NSW 2756, Australia
Printed and Bound in China
All Rights Reserved
Sterling ISBN 1-4027-1656-7

For information about custom editions, special sales, premium and corporate purchases, please contact Sterling Special Sales Department at 800-805-5489 or specialsales@sterlingpub.com

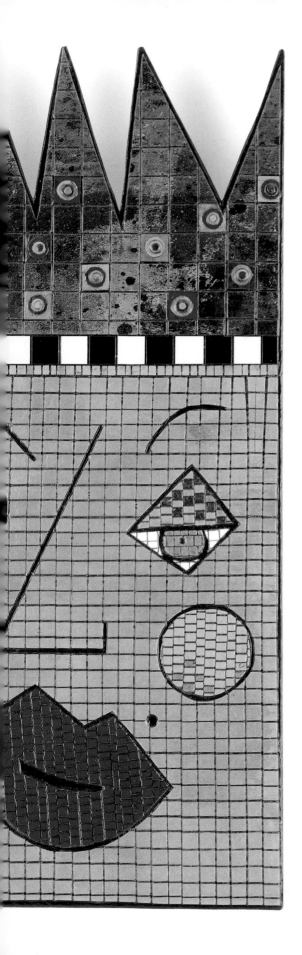

Contents

INTRODUCTION

As a professional artist, I travel around the United States, attending art fairs and festivals, selling my artwork to the public. When I first started, it was suggested that I put a sign in my booth saying "it's paper" to let people know my mosaic work is done completely in this medium. I considered it for a while, but ultimately decided against it for one reason: I enjoy seeing the look on people's faces when I tell them.

Typically this is what happens. A person walks into my booth and starts looking at my work. They reach out a hand to touch a table or mirror. I quietly say, "All my work is done with paper." They turn with furrowed brow and say "Paper??" I say, "Yes, paper." They say "No!" I say, "Yes!" This continues for several minutes until they believe me.

This conversation invariably leads to several questions. The first is, "How do you do this?" That is what this book is about. The second question is, "Are you the only person doing this?" to which I respond, "I hope not." I'm sure there are other artists out there who are playing with paper mosaic in unique ways, but I have not met them. I taught myself this art form and developed all the techniques found in this book. The third question that always comes up is, "How did you come up with this idea?" The answer to this question is a story of its own.

In 1998, my husband and I bought our first house and I began to decorate it. I have absolutely no training in art and the one drawing class that I ever signed up for I dropped halfway through because I was bored. However, like many of you reading this book, I have always been "crafty" and had a good eye for color and arrangement.

One of the first decorating projects in the house was upgrading our living-room furniture. Since we had spent our budget on the overstuffed sofa and chair, purchasing a coffee table and side table was out of the question. Not to be deterred from having a

6

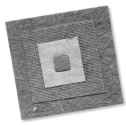

comfortable living room, I decided to make a coffee table myself. I purchased a wrought iron table base and a piece of plywood and made my first mosaic project from broken tile. I was hooked and quickly completed several more broken tile projects. However, I soon became frustrated with broken-tile mosaics because I could not control the color in the way I wanted and the pieces were heavy and brittle.

At about the same time, I had been experimenting with paper collage and was familiar with how paper hardened when saturated with acrylic medium. One day the idea hit me to cut up paper to look like broken tile, glue it down, and cover it in acrylic medium. The next day, I started a kitchen table project using this technique. I knew it would need to wear well, so after the acrylic medium dried, I applied four coats of polyurethane over it. That kitchen table has been used countless times by my family (which includes two small active boys) and continues to hold up beautifully.

Now, several years and several hundred projects later, I join you in these pages to introduce you to the attractive, fun, and flexible art of paper mosaic. I hope you enjoy designing, cutting, and gluing the mosaics as much as I do; and I hope the projects add beauty and artistic adventure to your life.

Why Paper Mosaic?

With limited time and a plethora of arts and crafts available to you, you might ask, "Why should I try paper mosaic?" You might even wonder if paper mosaic is the place to start for a novice mosaic artist. The truth is that paper mosaic is a great place to try mosaic for the first time, and the reasons for liking paper mosaic are plentiful.

Paper mosaic is "user friendly." Paper mosaic requires few tools, the materials are inexpensive, and a simple project can be started and finished in a couple of hours. However, it must also be said that paper mosaic is an elegant and flexible medium that can be used to create extraordinary works of art. Because of the flexibility of this medium,

Introduction continued

you may find yourself starting a simple project today, but moving into more-complex designs in the years to come.

Paper mosaic is forgivable. If you make a mistake, you can peel away the tile and reglue another. Also, because you can paint paper to match a specific color palette, you can try many times to get the exact color. Your only expense in making a mistake is the cost of paint and paper.

Paper mosaic is extremely functional. It is lightweight, thin, and is water resistant when covered with acrylic medium and urethane. With tile mosaic, your projects will be thick, heavy, and brittle. Furthermore, paper mosaic captures the look of tile mosaic, yet allows you the flexibility of decorating objects such as journals, light switch covers, ornaments, or tables.

Paper mosaic is fun. You are not limited in color or the supplies that you must purchase from someone else just paint a piece a paper and start a project. It's fun because it's a new art form. It often takes a while to convince someone that it really is paper. Why? Because paper mosaic doesn't look like paper, and that's fun too!

I hope that as you look at these pages, you will find the inspiration to give paper mosaic a try. If you do, I think you will find a beautiful, fun, and flexible medium with which to decorate your life.

Book Overview

This book is organized into three sections that will familiarize you with the art of paper mosaic. The first section introduces you to basic techniques and concepts, including the materials and tools you'll need to get started. The next section teaches ten techniques using projects that build on previous skills learned. Photographs and written descriptions of additional projects demonstrate the flexibility and scope of each technique. The final section showcases several mosaic projects to inspire you to use paper mosaic in unique and challenging ways.

The book is designed sequentially: each project builds on skills learned in previous projects. I would therefore suggest that the projects be completed in order, as each project provides valuable learning opportunities. Once you have mastered the ten techniques in this book, the sky is the limit for you and your paper mosaic designs.

Design Considerations

I think it is important for you to know that this art form is evolving. The directions in this book are comprehensive enough to comfortably take you from the start to the finish of each project. However, I have tried to leave some of the design choices (such as color selection) up to you. Remember, the projects are designed to teach you techniques. How you stylize and apply the techniques is up to you.

To assist you, particularly in the beginning, I have included "Artist Tips" throughout the book. These are things I have learned in the years of working with paper mosaic. Some of the tips are specific to techniques and will help you master some of the technical aspects of paper mosaic. Other tips regard design considerations such as color selection, tile placement, and the use of

Introduction continued

texture. Hopefully, these tips will help you gain confidence in your early work in paper mosaic. However, keep in mind that rules about art are meant to be broken.

It is my hope that as you become increasingly familiar with paper mosaic, you will begin to create new and interesting applications. In the art world this is called, "Finding your voice" and is what defines your art as uniquely your own. When we first start out, we must copy to gain understanding – just as you will do in completing the projects in this book. However, we must eventually experiment and play with the medium until it takes on our own personality. So have fun with color, trust your gut when it comes to design, and never, ever let fear or doubt into your studio.

Acknowledgements

Artwork does not evolve, a business does not succeed and a book is not written without assistance. I am grateful to many people who have supported the development of my work.

My thanks to the staff of Chapelle, Ltd., for their hard work in making this book a reality. In particular, I thank Jo Packham for believing in my artwork, and Matthew DeMaio for making it look beautiful on these pages.

At pivotal points in my career, Colleen Cowhy and Tommy Youngblood encouraged me to "take it to the next level." Angie Price and Morag Totten, the two best mentors an artist could have, shared resources and reassured me after "failures." Annette Velarde, my dearest friend, kept me sane during the early years with her humor, compassion, and grappa.

My brother and his family have supported me with their prayers. My father, a patent attorney and entrepreneur advocate, has given me invaluable business advice. He and his wife have proven themselves to be tireless in the support of my business and family, for which I am grateful. Our two sons, Zachary and Noble, remain the motivation for continuing my art business—I am thankful for their patience, their art appreciation, and for having them in my life.

This book is dedicated to my mother and my husband, both of whom have gone the extra mile for me throughout the life of my business. My mother gave up her dining room and garage and watched my children so my husband and I could attend art fairs. She never complained and never stopped believing in me. Her steadfastness and support has been a model for me as a mother.

My beloved husband became the chief cook, nanny, housekeeper, errand boy, gardener, and social coordinator for our family. He has also played important roles in my art business by finishing pieces, constructing my Web site and attending art shows. It has been my privilege to be married to him for over thirteen years. He is my best friend, my strongest supporter, and the person I am most grateful to walk through life with. Thank-you Patrick, for showing me the art of love.

CHAPTER ONE

Paper Mosaic Basics

Section 1: Getting started

In many ways, paper mosaic is similar to its traditional cousin, but in other ways it is quite different. Like traditional mosaic, paper mosaic needs a form, or base, onto which the tiles are adhered to. It also requires tiles and tile adhesives. A major difference is that paper mosaic requires no grouting; it mimics traditional mosaic by providing a raised surface (paper backed with posterboard) and lines (the space between paper tiles) that give the illusion of grouting.

This illusion is further enhanced by the application of acrylic medium to the paper tiles, which soaks into the paper and changes its properties. Acrylic-coated paper can look like ceramic, linoleum, or even leather.

In this section, we will discuss the materials and tools needed to create paper mosaic projects. There are few expensive or specialized tools needed to create these projects; most of what is needed to get started can be found around your home. However, as you create more projects, you may want to invest in a few things, such as a cutting grid and rotary cutter, that will make your experience with paper mosaic easier and more enjoyable.

Mosaic Forms

A mosaic form is the base onto which you apply tiles. Because paper mosaic is lightweight and the thickness of the tiles is less that 1/32", a wide variety of forms are amenable to paper mosaic application. The only limitation is that these forms must be rigid and porous.

A rigid form is important because bending a form will cause cracking in the acrylic medium. Keep in mind that thickness does not necessarily dictate rigidity. Several of the projects in this book are completed on thin forms such as journal covers and foam-core board. Even though these materials are thin, they do not bend easily and are therefore suitable for paper mosaic application.

A porous form absorbs fluids. The porosity of a form is important because it must be able to

ARTIST'S TIP:

Several projects in this book use ready-made, unfinished wooden forms such as picture frames and serving trays. Unfinished wooden forms can be found in craft stores and provide inexpensive bases for paper mosaics without having to construct them yourself.

absorb the glue that adheres the paper tiles. Because paper mosaics lack the grout that helps hold traditional mosaic tiles into place, it is extremely important that the tiles adhere firmly to the base. Highly porous materials such as foam-core, mat board, cardboard, and wood make excellent bases for paper mosaics; non-porous forms made of glass and metal make poor bases. Plastics and Formica can be used for paper mosaics if you take some preparatory steps, which will be covered later in this section.

Wooden Forms

Wood is an excellent base material for paper mosaics. It is inexpensive, rigid, and easy to cut and paint. I use 1" pine and ¼" hardboard to build clocks, mirrors, and other projects. For tables and game boards, I use ¾" plywood.

Wood forms

Guidelines for choosing wood:

- Always choose well-cured wood that is free from large knots, mildew, and warping.

- If you choose green (uncured) wood, it may warp after you have completed the project and crack the acrylic finish.

- If you own a saw, you can cut your own forms. If you don't have any woodworking equipment, you can find a large variety of unfinished wooden projects at your local craft store or unfinished furniture store.

- New, unfinished wood is the easiest to prepare. However, salvaged furniture or wooden pieces can also be considered.

- If using old wood, it must be solid and free from large holes and cracks. Small holes, cracks, and scratches can be filled with wood putty, but large fissures will undermine the structural integrity of the paper mosaic.

Paper Forms

Cardboard, mat board, and foam-core board are acceptable forms for paper mosaics, although each has its advantages and disadvantages as a base.

Paper forms

Cardboard is easy to cut, readily available and often free; but it bends easily and requires painting. If you choose cardboard, use the double-corrugated variety or glue two or more pieces together.

Mat board is the thinnest paper product I use for paper mosaics, but it is quite sturdy and comes in a variety of colors. Scrap mat board can often be obtained from artists or framing shops; even scratched or damaged boards can be used. The disadvantage of using mat boards is that the thicker ones are sometimes difficult to cut.

Foam-core board is my product of choice when using paper products to create forms. It is lightweight, easy to cut, and sturdy. I use black foam-core board so I don't have to paint it prior to starting my mosaic projects. Foam-core board can be painted, so if you can only find white, build the form, then color it with acrylic paint.

I like the thickness of foam-core board: typically ⅜"—just enough to provide a nice edge for gluing when constructing boxes or other forms. Foam-core board is expensive. You should be able to find it at a craft supply store, but it is several dollars for a 24" x 36" sheet. Sometimes I can find black foam-core board at office supply stores for a reasonable price.

Plastic and Formica Forms

Many plastic forms can be used in paper mosaics with great success. Project 10, for example, shows how to decorate plastic switch plate covers. Because plastic is rigid, it is usually acceptable even though it is not as porous as paper or wood. Formica is another surface that can be used for paper mosaics .I have completed several Formica paper mosaic countertops with great success. The biggest problem with plastic and Formica forms is that paint scratches off them easily, this can be addressed by rough sanding and priming these surfaces prior to painting them. These processes will be covered in detail in the next section.

Plastic forms

Form Preparation Tips:

- Make sure that each form is clean, dry, and free from structural disintegration.

- If paint is flaking or wood is chipping, the piece must be sanded and repaired before continuing with the project.

- If you are using a piece of furniture that has been previously painted, it may not be necessary for you to repaint it. However, you must check the quality of the paint job and determine if it will provide a sound base for the paper tiles.

- If the piece has a high-gloss finish, use sandpaper to roughen the surface you are planning to mosaic. A slightly roughened surface will increase the strength of the bond between the form and the paper tile once the tiles have been glued into place.

Form Preparation

In writing this book, I wanted to offer a wide range of projects, some of which have forms constructed from wood. If you have experience in a wood shop, building these forms will pose no challenge: you will already be familiar with the tools and processes required. For those of you with no experience or access to woodworking tools, I have included alternative directions for the construction of forms from foam-core board.

Form preparation tools

Filling Holes

When dealing with wooden forms, it's important to check for small holes, cracks, or fissures in the wood; even a small hole will become exaggerated when the piece is painted. Fill each hole and crack with sandable wood filler. Small holes can be filled in, using your finger; larger cracks require a putty knife to make the fill even with the surrounding surface. After the putty has dried, sand the wooden form with medium-grit sandpaper to smooth away splinters and rough edges.

Wood fill and sanding materials

Sanding

Typically, light sanding with medium-grit sandpaper is sufficient to prepare wooden forms for painting and mosaic surfacing. However, if you are dealing with fine furniture, you may want to thoroughly sand the parts of the furniture that will not be covered by paper tile. For example, if you're preparing a table, you should fine-sand the legs, but keep the tabletop rough so the paper tiles will adhere better. If you are working with plastic or Formica forms, use a course-grit sandpaper to roughen the surface. Use a damp cloth to wipe sawdust from the forms before continuing to the priming and painting phase of form preparation.

Priming and Painting

Once the forms have been filled, sanded, and cleaned, you are ready to prime and paint them. I am not particular about primer or paint and tend to use inexpensive, readily available, spray-can varieties. The main thing to remember is to let the primer dry completely before painting,

Priming and painting supplies

to avoid extremes in temperature, and to apply any spray-can product in a well-ventilated area. Also, I should state that all of my bases are painted black before I mosaic them. This is strictly my personal preference and in no way should be interpreted as the only or right way to do paper mosaics. Remember, that the color of the paint is the color of the grout on the finished project. Let your imagination and creativity dictate what color you paint the forms.

Choosing and Using Papers

Entire books have been written about paper-making and paper painting; and frankly, I could write pages about the beautiful papers available for paper mosaics. However, I will limit the scope of this section to general descriptions of papers and their unique applications to paper mosaics. If you are a paper lover as I am, I encourage you to scour the craft stores and the Internet for different papers and paper-painting techniques that will make your project the unique personal expression that you mean it to be.

Handmade Papers

Several years ago, I explored papermaking with the help of my blender and botanicals from my backyard. I had fun, but quickly determined that I prefer cutting up paper more than I like pulping and pouring it. Fortunately, there are wonderful handmade papers available at paper stores or for sale over the Internet. The list of my favorites is too large to list, but there are several properties that you should consider when making your choice.

ARTIST'S TIP:

Handmade paper can change dramatically in appearance once it is saturated in decoupage medium. Typically, colors will darken and inclusions (leaves and fibers that are typical of handmade paper) will become more prominent. Test papers by gluing a small section of paper to posterboard, then saturating it with decoupage medium. When it dries, see whether the new color is acceptable to you.

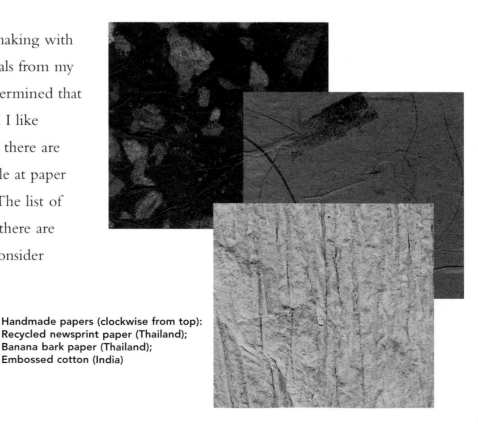

Handmade papers (clockwise from top):
Recycled newsprint paper (Thailand);
Banana bark paper (Thailand);
Embossed cotton (India)

Some considerations for choosing handmade paper:

- Many handmade-paper dyes fade, but some fade more than others. With some mango leaf papers made in Thailand, for example, the purple fades terribly but the reds stay true. Yet on some mulberry papers, the reds fade. Each paper behaves differently, but generally purples, blues, reds, and bright greens (such as teal) tend to fade more than others. I no longer purchase handmade papers in these colors. I paint papers with acrylic paint in these shades because I have found that acrylic paint is most resistant to fading. Nonetheless, handmade papers are so beautiful and add such wonderful texture to a piece that I use them whenever I can. Many papers, particularly those in the earth tones, hold up beautifully and are well worth the investment.

- When you apply decoupage medium to handmade papers, fibers will sometimes move around. This isn't necessarily a problem—you just might not like the look. Pay attention when you apply the medium: use small brush strokes and wipe away any fibers that stray too far from home.

- Most of the professionally made paper imported from overseas is quite thin, which makes it easy to glue to a backing paper and cut. However, sometimes it is so thin that its color changes dramatically when a decoupage medium is applied. This happens because the color of the posterboard shows through the thin paper. Sometimes this creates a beautiful mottled effect. Other times, it can ruin a piece. If you are concerned, test a piece by gluing a small section of paper to posterboard, then saturating it. When the decoupage medium dries, see whether the color it produces is acceptable to you.

- Occasionally I use thicker pulped and poured papers. They are typically natural in color and contain a variety of botanicals such as straw, tea leaves, and flower petals. They're much thicker than the papers I usually use, which makes them more difficult to cut. But the results are extraordinary; because the paper is natural in color and the surface is bumpy and uneven, the final mosaic resembles stone. If you have a stack of handmade papers in your basement left over from your experiments with pulping and pouring, pull them out and try them in your paper mosaic projects.

Printed and Colored Papers

Printed and colored papers such as those found in scrapbooking stores work wonderfully in paper mosaics. They come in a wide variety of colors and are largely fade resistant. Choose printed papers with small and simple patterns; sometimes what is wonderful on a 12" square sheet is lost when cut into small squares. Choose papers with interesting colors and textures; these will translate even if you only see a small piece.

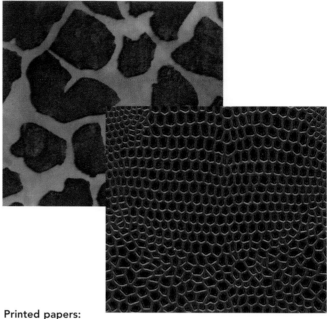

**Printed papers:
Giraffe and lizard skin**

ARTIST'S TIP:

Texture is the variation of color or surface of paper. When choosing printed papers such as those found in scrapbooking stores, look for papers with a small even texture. These will add visual interest to the work without overwhelming it. Also, keep in mind that too much texture can make a piece look busy. Combine textures and solids for a nice effect.

Painted Papers

I like to paint most of my papers and when I have time, I love to play with painting techniques. There are wonderful books on painting decorative papers. If you're inclined, explore this area. Hand-painted paper techniques include marbling, pulled paste, batik, and faux finish. Any technique that you've used to paint your walls, such as sponging, ragging, or feather painting, can be easily translated to paper. If you

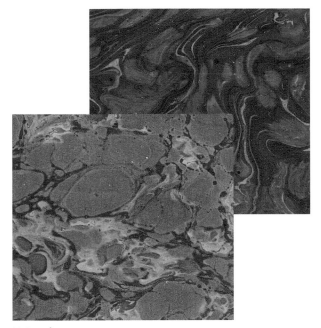

Painted papers:
Red and green marbled

Miscellaneous Papers

Almost any paper can be used for paper mosaics with a few exceptions. Tissue wrapping paper, recycled artwork, cardstock, and watercolor paper are all acceptable choices if you keep in mind that they may react uniquely to the decoupage medium. You can always test a patch using the following method:

1. Using spray glue, glue a 2" x 4" piece of paper onto black posterboard.

2. Brush decoupage medium over the piece of paper.

3. Once the medium has dried, cut the piece in half. Place a 2" square section in a window sill that gets a lot of sun and place the other in a drawer.

4. Compare the two pieces after a day or so. If you have a lot of fading on the paper exposed to the sun, you may want to choose another paper (unless you like the look of the faded paper.)

I encourage you to avoid newsprint, magazine or other glossy-printed materials, along with children's construction paper. The quality of the paper is poor and fading is extreme.

have limited time and want to get straight to the business of paper mosaics, look for painted papers in your local art store. Hand-marbled papers from France and Italy are extraordinary and far beyond my own modest marbling skills. I find that it is worth purchasing these papers because they add such elegance to my paper mosaic projects.

Paper Preparation

Throughout this book, I will be asking you to prepare papers for mosaic projects by backing them with posterboard. The posterboard thickens the paper and gives it the dimension that is unique to paper mosaics. Without the posterboard backing, the paper tiles would have little relief and resemble paper collage more than mosaic. Backing the papers is therefore an important step to producing the paper mosaic look.

Materials for paper preparation

The reason I choose black posterboard is because I work on black forms. This is a personal preference, not a rule. You may back the papers in whatever color posterboard you

choose. Although you could use another type of paper for backing, such as watercolor paper or cardstock, it's not usually advisable to do so. Cardstock is usually too thin. Watercolor paper is too expensive. However, if you are using old watercolor paintings in the mosaic designs, they will not need to be backed. Professional watercolor paper is thick enough to be used for paper mosaics as is.

The easiest way to back papers in preparation for mosaic projects is as follows:

1. Cut sheets from the mosaic paper and poster-board that are approximately the same size. I suggest 12" square because it is an easy size to manage and is easy to cut with a rotary cutter and cutting grid.

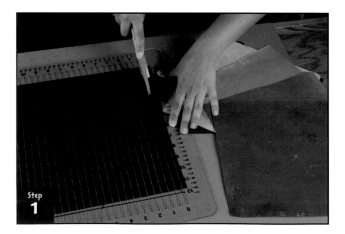

Step 1

2. Place the sheet of paper, colored side down, next to the posterboard.

3. Spray the backs of both sheets with a high-quality spray glue, to ensure a good bond between paper and posterboard.

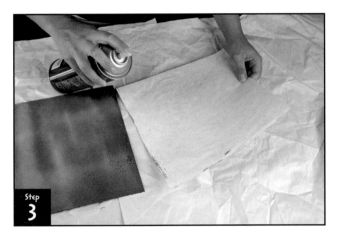

5. Use a brayer or a rolling pin to roll out any air bubbles or wrinkles.

The paper is now ready to be cut up and used in mosaic projects.

4. Flip the posterboard over, onto the paper, glued sides together.

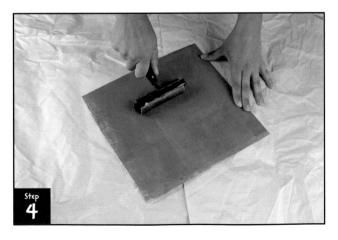

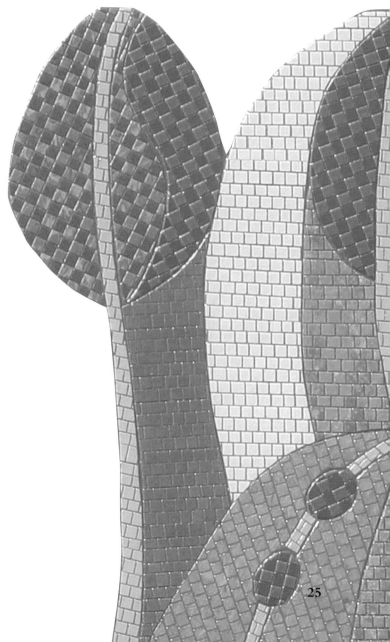

25

Cutting Tools

There are very few cutting tools needed to get started in paper mosaic. A good, sharp pair of scissors is essential: several projects in this book can be completed with nothing more. Another necessary tool, particularly if you are cutting foam-core board, is a wallpaper knife. Wallpaper knives are similar to retractable-blade box cutters, but they are smaller and have thinner blades. They are inexpensive, readily available at hardware stores, and they cut easily through foam-core board.

Paper cutting tools

A straightedge, preferably a metal ruler, is necessary to use with wallpaper cutters.

I recommend a metal ruler because the blade of the wallpaper cutter will not damage it and you will find many uses for it in your studio.

The more advanced projects in this book require precision cutting. This is most easily achieved with a rotary cutting system. The rotary system is often used in quilting and is comprised of three essential components: the cutting mat, the cutting grid, and the rotary cutter.

A cutting mat is a thin plastic sheet that is resistant to gouging by sharp blades. It does not dull the rotary cutter, as other surfaces will. The mats come in a variety of sizes. I recommend a mat at least 18" square so that the rotary cutting grid fits comfortably within its perimeter. The cutting grid I use is a 12"-square plastic sheet with slots every ½" inch. These slots provide an easy and accurate way to cut paper in ½" increments.

Rotary cutting blades are round and attach to a plastic handle that rotates like a wheel. The rotary cutter goes into the slots on the cutting grid. As you push down and move the cutter, the blade cuts the paper.

Paper Adhesives

There are many types of adhesives available. Artists typically choose them, based on whether or not they are archival. Non-archival glues discolor or negatively effect the artwork over time. To be honest, I've never worried about this with paper mosaic for several reasons. First, the paper is saturated in decoupage medium; using archival glue under the paper when the surface is coated with decoupage medium and polyurethane seems silly. Second, paper mosaics are meant to be used. It is my hope that your projects show damage only after years of use.

My recommendations for glues are simple. Any white craft glue is appropriate for adhering tiles to their forms. You can also use decoupage medium to glue tiles down. However, both white glue and decoupage medium are very wet and take a long time to dry. This is fine if you need more time to position tiles. However, as you get faster with the layout, you may want to switch to tacky glue: a thicker form of white glue which sticks to the tiles better and dries faster. I apply glue to the forms with an inexpensive 1" paintbrush purchased at a home building center.

The other type of glue you will need for the paper mosaic projects is good-quality spray glue. Spray glue is used to attach the paper to its backing prior to cutting it into tiles. You can use a white glue for this; but it's messy, takes more time, and tends to buckle the paper.

When using spray glue to attach papers to posterboard, you will want to apply a thin coat to both the posterboard and the back of the paper before sandwiching them together.

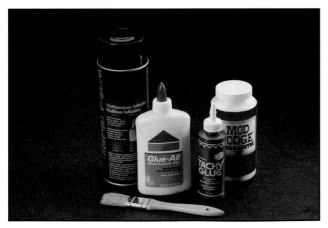

Paper adhesives

Coating the backs of both will ensure proper bonding. Sometimes, after you have glued the papers to the backing, you will have separation. If this happens, change the brand of spray glue and reseal the papers with a thin coat of white glue. It is very important that the papers stay glued to the posterboard backing, or you will have problems later when you are cutting and gluing the paper tiles onto forms. So take this step very seriously and purchase good-quality spray glue.

However, if you want to avoid spray glues, brush a thin coat of white glue (tacky glue is too thick) onto a piece of posterboard. Place the paper, good side up, onto the posterboard and smooth out any bubbles or wrinkles with a brayer or rolling pin. Let the paper dry; and if it buckles, place it under a piece of Plexiglas and place weights on top.

Some of the projects in this book require you to construct forms from wood or foam-core board. When constructing or repairing wooden forms, use a good-quality wood glue to ensure a tight, long-lasting bond. If you construct the forms with foam-core board, you may use either craft glue or a hot-glue gun. Hot-glue guns have an advantage because they can assemble forms quickly due to the short amount of time it takes for hot glue to harden. However, please be careful when using hot-glue guns because you can get burned very quickly.

Sealing and Protecting Mosaics

Once you have completed the adhesion of paper tiles to a form, it must be sealed with some type of medium that will soak into the papers and harden them. There are many types of acrylic mediums available at art supply stores, and they all have unique properties.

However, for the purposes of this book, we will use decoupage medium because it is readily

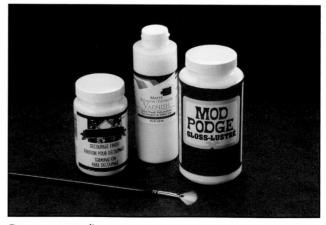

Decoupage medium

available and will give satisfactory results in all of the projects. Decoupage medium is similar to acrylic medium in that it dries hard and clear; but it is very inexpensive compared to acrylic mediums and can be purchased at a variety of stores. If you are an artist with a particular affinity for a brand of acrylic medium, then by all means use it and let me know if you find any advantages.

Decoupage medium comes in different brands with different finishes. You will have to explore the different brands available to you and decide which one you prefer. Avoid brands that cloud and create excessive bubbles when brushed onto the project. Sometimes clouding and bubbling can differ between finishes, even though they are the same brand. For example, I use a brand of decoupage medium with a matte finish for many of my projects. One day the store was out of the matte finish so I purchased the same brand but in a gloss finish. I was surprised to see how many more bubbles the gloss medium produced when brushed onto the project. I spent more time than I wanted brushing out bubbles, and have not bought the gloss finish since.

Acrylic and decoupage mediums should be applied to the projects with a good-quality brush. I use a fan shaped-brush that does a nice job moving the medium around the project without leaving obvious brush strokes. When choosing a brush, choose a soft-bristle brush with a width of at least ¾" but not more than 1½". The brush should be clean and sound, not leaving flecks of paint or brush bristles floating in the decoupage medium.

After the decoupage medium has dried on the pieces, I recommend the application of polyurethane. This step is not strictly necessary unless the piece is a table or something that will hang in a moist environment such as a bathroom. However, I find that the urethane adds a nice finish and can provide protection against ultraviolet damage. For wall pieces or work that will not be exposed to a lot of moisture, a light coat of U.V.-resistant polyurethane from a spray can is sufficient.

Polyurethane comes in a variety of finishes such a satin, semigloss, and high gloss. Try the different finishes and choose the one that suits you and the personality of your projects. Remember to follow the manufacturer's directions on the can and to apply all urethanes in well-ventilated areas.

If you are making a paper mosaic table or a piece that will have a lot of wear and tear, you need to apply polyurethane in liquid form with

Polyurethane sealers

a sponge roller. Sponge rollers are inexpensive and work better that nap rollers because they leave fewer fibers in the polyurethane. However, any time you roll on a finish, you will need to look closely for bits and pieces that

ARTIST'S TIP:

I have yet to find a urethane that does not yellow, even if the can says "non-yellowing." In general, this doesn't bother me because the slight yellowing gives a beautiful patina to the tables and pure whites end up looking buttery. I adjust my color palette in advance, knowing there will be yellowing, then go ahead with the project. Pure whites are easier to obtain in projects that only require a light coating of urethane from a can. However, any project that needs two or more thick coats of urethane will show some yellowing, so keep this in mind when designing your color palettes.

have decided to join the artwork without invitation. Pet hairs, dust bunnies, mosquitoes, and sponge chunks have all made their way into my artwork from time to time, so be vigilant. To ensure lasting wear on tables, I recommend at

chunks have all made their way into my artwork from time to time, so be vigilant. To ensure lasting wear on tables, I recommend at least four coats of urethane with ample drying time between each coat. You can keep the sponge roller in a plastic bag in the fridge between coats (longer than two days it will start to dry out), but you should throw it away after applying the final coat. Cleaning the sponge with mineral spirits disintegrates the material and leaves it unsuitable for future use.

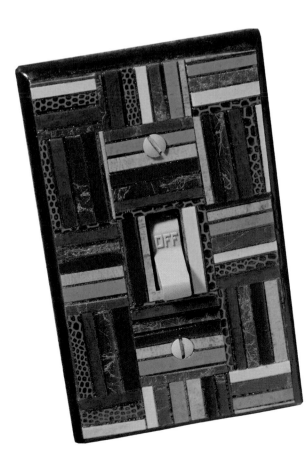

Miscellaneous Materials, Tips, and Techniques

As a busy mom, wife, and artist, it is essential that things are as easy and convenient for me as possible when working on my projects. Over the years, I have developed a few practices that help me save time and mistakes. The first tip I have is the use of Plexiglas: one of the most

A project loaded on a piece of plexiglass

important tools in my studio. I use various sizes of Plexiglas sheets for a variety of purposes. In painting papers, I use them under my projects to protect countertops from paint smears and splatters. Some of my Plexiglas sheets have been used for so many years, and have so much paint on them; they have become works of art

31

themselves! I also use Plexiglas sheets to weight papers down. If I'm working on a project and the edges of some of my tiles start to curl (which is almost always) I use small pieces of Plexiglas and canned goods to weight down a section while I work on another section. Plexiglas sheets are extremely handy when I am

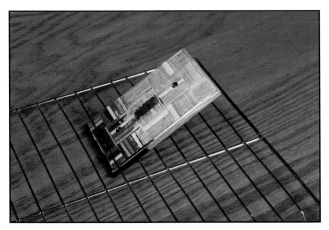

Drying rack for small projects

laying out a piece. I'll carry a large piece of Plexiglas (24" x 36") with all my tiles and project components into the kitchen so I can stir a pot of soup or oversee lunch for my children. If things get hectic, I simply take the piece of Plexiglas back into my studio and leave it. For those of you with limited space and no dedicated studio, this provides an alternative to

spending time getting things out and putting them away every day, which takes too much time away from actually creating. Try to find a place to store your Plexiglas sheet (like under a

Drying cans for large projects

bed), load it with the mosaic project and get it out when you have a few minutes. When creative time is up, put it away until the next time you have a few minutes. Using this technique, I have been known to convert any room in my house into a mosaic studio in a matter of seconds. My husband jokes that I don't just have one studio in the house, but that every room in our house is my studio. True, very true.

Applying decoupage medium to a project and having it dry without smears and scuffs can be a challenge. I use a few readily found kitchen items to help me avoid problems. For thin mosaic projects such as magnets, coasters, trivets, ornaments, and night-lights, I use a cookie-cooling rack to prop up the project as it dries. Typically, I will apply decoupage medium to the top half of the project, front and back, then prop it in the rack to dry. Later I will repeat the project for the lower half.

For larger projects such as serving trays, picture frames, and clocks, I use canned goods to keep the project off the counter while I apply decoupage medium to the top and sides. It is also a good idea to place a piece of Plexiglas under any project you are applying medium to, so that drips and spills land on the Plexiglas rather than the countertop.

CHAPTER TWO
Techniques

SECTION 2

DIRECT APPLICATION MOSAICS

In paper mosaics, there are two ways to apply paper tiles. The direct application of tiles is a method that will be familiar to traditional mosaic artists because it follows the traditional steps of cutting tiles and gluing them into place. In projects 1–6, we will explore how this traditional method can be used with paper tiles and some variations that are unique to paper. However, you can cut them and apply them directly to mosaic forms, or you can create sheets of paper you can use for future projects. Creating these mosaic sheets is a method specific to paper mosaic and will be covered in projects 7–10.

Technique 1
USING SQUARES & RECTANGLES

This first technique is the simplest of paper mosaic applications. It teaches you to create designs and color patterns using simple squares and rectangles. It also introduces you to the core concepts of paper mosaic: creating tiles, preparing forms, gluing tiles, and finishing projects.

Five-color Tea Tray

Step 1

Prepare an unfinished tray (these can be found in craft stores) for painting by filling small holes with wood fill and sanding rough edges.

Step 2

Prime and paint the tray black, let dry.

ARTIST'S TIP:

When choosing colors for this project, use either a palette of similar colors such as five shades of green, or very different colors such as the ones I have used. Try to keep all of the colors either warm or cool. If you mix warm and cool tones, the project can look muddy.

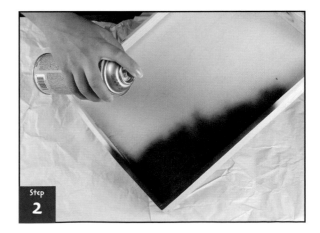

Step 3

Either paint papers in five colors or purchase printed, colored, or handmade paper. Cut these papers into 12" squares.

Step 4

Cut black posterboard in 12"-square sheets. Spray a piece of posterboard and the back of one of the pieces of paper with spray glue.

Step 5

Sandwich the glued sides of the paper together and using a brayer (or a rolling pin if you don't have a brayer), smooth out any bubbles or wrinkles.

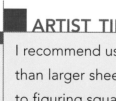

ARTIST TIP:

I recommend using 12"-square sections of paper because they are easier to handle than larger sheets, fit perfectly within a rotary cutting grid, and lend themselves nicely to figuring square-inch coverage for projects. For example, a 3'-square table would use nine 12"-square sheets of paper.

Step 6

Using either a cutting grid with a rotary cutter or scissors, cut the posterboard-backed paper into 1" squares. If you are using scissors, I recommend that you use a pencil and straightedge to mark a cutting edge. Try to get the tiles as square as possible. If they are not square, you will have trouble laying out the project and may have to do a lot of trimming. Repeat Steps 4–6 for all the papers.

Step 7

Using a ruler, locate the center of the tray and draw a + lightly in pencil.

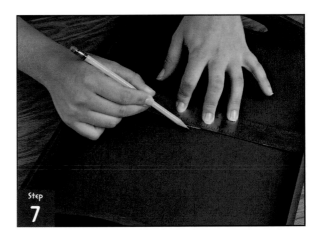

Step 8

With a brush, apply a thin layer of glue in the lower-right corner of the + and place a tile.

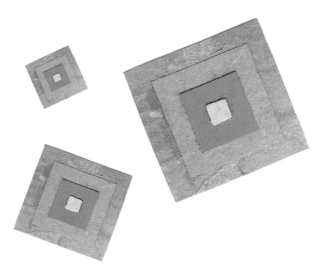

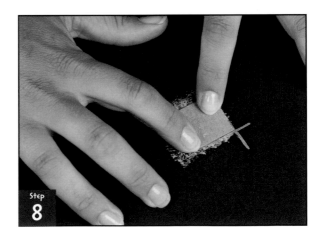

Step 9

Using the first tile as a guide, continue to apply glue and then tiles, working from the center out. Leave approximately a ½2" space between the tiles. Alternate colors so that you have a nice color balance throughout the piece. Keep the tile in a straight line. When applying the second row of tiles, center the tiles between the tiles in the row above. The tiles will be stair-stepped.

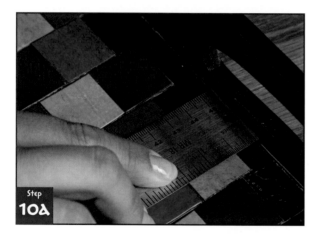

Step 10

When you get to the edges and can no longer place 1" tiles, use a ruler to measure the space between the edge of the tray and the edge of the tile. Subtract ½2" from the measurement (you need this for the space between tiles), cut the tile, and glue it into place. Repeat this process until the entire edge of the project is filled in.

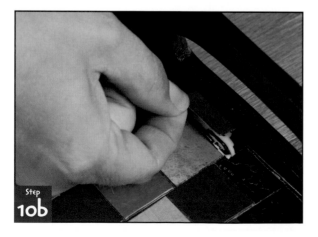

Step 11

Make sure all the tiles are glued down and the glue has had time to dry. Brush the entire surface of tiles with a thin coat of decoupage medium. Brush out any bubbles that appear and use a toothpick to push down any troublesome corners that pop up. Let the medium dry, keeping an eye out for bubbles and lifting corners.

Step 12

Spray the entire project with polyurethane and let it dry.

Step 13

Glue feet to the tray if desired. The feet shown here are 1"-square blocks glued with leftover tiles from the project. Also, I glued small squares of colored tile to edges of the piece to add a little interesting detail.

Tissue Box Covers

The boxes on these two pages were decorated using the same applications learned in Five-color Tea Tray on pages 38–43. The tissue box at right is identical in technique to the tea tray; but rather than using 1" squares, I have used ½" squares. The box at lower right uses 1" x ½" rectangles and ½" squares in contrasting colors to create the illusion of basket weave. The tissue box on page 44 was created using a variety squares and rectangles in different colors placed in a random pattern.

■ **ARTIST'S TIP:**

The paper used in the top-right tissue box was faux-painted to create texture. This paper was painted with a sponge, using several colors to create the illusion of movement. Printed papers can also be textured. Look for small even textures that add visual interest without being overwhelming.

45

The following instructions will assist you in making tissue-box covers. Use the same directions for Five-color Tea Tray on pages 40–43 (changing the size of tiles if desired) to cover the boxes.

Step 1

Using ⅜" black foam-core board and a wall-paper knife, cut four 4¾" x 5¼" rectangles. Cut one 5" square. Note: Wallpaper knives are similar to box cutters, but with thin, retractable, snap-off blades. Their small size makes them ideal for cutting foam-core board.

Step 2

Glue the four 4¾" x 5" rectangles together into a box. Glue along the 5" side as shown in the photograph at left.

Step 3

Cut a 2"-square opening in the center of the 5" square. This leaves a 1½" border around the edge.

Step 4

Glue the top onto the box. Decorate as desired.

Chessboard This chessboard is a simple plywood square that was designed with the same application learned in Five-color Tea Tray on pages 40–43, with a few differences. The 1" squares that make up the playing area don't have space between them. The border and edging are a random placement of squares and rectangles in a variety of colors. The height of the edging on the chessboard is dependent on the thickness of the plywood used to construct the base. Cut the thickness of the tiles ⅛" less than the thickness of the plywood.

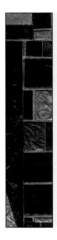

Technique 2
DIRECT APPLICATION OF RANDOMLY CUT TILES

In the previous projects, you learned how to apply square and rectangular tiles. Technique 2 is different because you will be using randomly cut tiles. The look of these projects is similar to broken-tile mosaic and is more free form in its application.

Journal with Leaf Pattern

Step
1

Step 1

Use a wire-bound journal with a thick cover for this project. Journals can be found in most craft supply stores. With a pencil, draw a simple leaf shape on the front cover of the journal.

◼ ARTIST'S TIP:

You won't need much paper for this project, but throughout the book I ask that you work with 12"-square sheets. If you are painting papers, this is an easy size to handle. If you don't use it all for one project, it's nice to have the paper available for other projects. Scrapbooking stores sell beautiful papers in this size. There is nothing worse than running out of paper in the middle of a project, so always prepare more than enough—you can always use it later.

Step 2

Paint a 12"-square sheet of paper green and another yellow, or use handmade or printed papers.

Step 3

Use spray glue to attach black posterboard to the back of the green and yellow papers. Smooth out bubbles and wrinkles with a brayer or rolling pin.

Step 4

Randomly cut tiles the approximate size of a dime, but with a variety of shapes and sizes. Imagine what broken tiles or plates look like and try to mimic their shape.

Step 5

Brush glue inside the penciled leaf shape on the journal and randomly place the cut green tiles. Feel free to trim the tiles as you place them, but don't get too exact. Remember, this is supposed to look like broken tile mosaic—grout lines are not even or symmetrical. Leave a slightly wider space down the center of the leaf so that it looks like the leaf's vein.

Step 6

Let the green leaf tiles dry, then carefully apply a thin coat of glue around the leaf design. Be careful to avoid getting glue on the green tiles.

Step 7

Fill in the area around the leaf with the yellow tiles. Leave a 3/16" border free from tile at the edge of the journal and in front of the wire binding. Let the glue dry completely.

Step 8

Brush decoupage medium over the entire cover, being careful to avoid the wire binding. Let the medium dry.

Step 9

Spray the journal cover with polyurethane and let it dry.

ARTIST'S TIP:

If the journal cover curls slightly after the decoupage medium has dried, don't panic. As the medium cures (over a period of five to seven days) it should flatten back out. If it doesn't, set a few heavy books on it (careful not to bend the wire binding) and let it set for a week.

Step 6

Step 7

Step 8

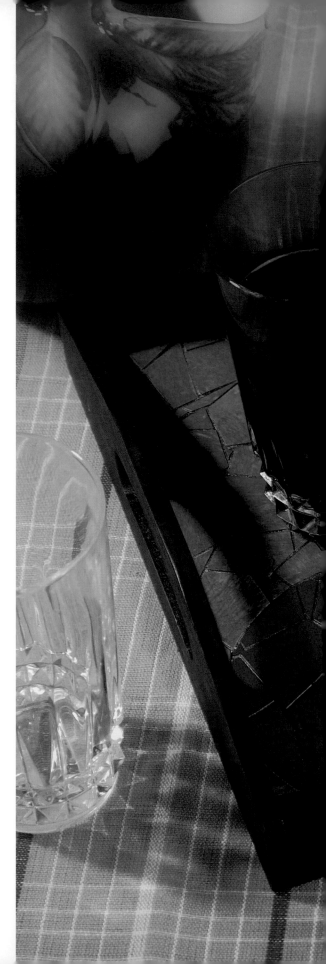

Abstract Fruit Serving Tray

This photograph shows a serving tray that was made using the same design application in Journal with Leaf Pattern on pages 48–51. It has more colors, but the placement of randomly cut tiles is the same. When doing a more complicated design such as this one, I suggest sketching out the design several times before committing. Think about shape and balance of color when creating the designs. Also, simple designs with clean lines and little detail work best with this style of mosaic. When you are happy with the design, use transfer paper to transfer the design onto the tray.

Technique 3
COMBINING LINEAR & NONLINEAR DESIGNS

In previous techniques, you learned to create tight designs with squares and rectangles placed close together and loose designs with randomly cut and placed tiles. Technique 3 combines both types of tiles and will also show how to trim around curves and tight spaces. You will need a burnishing tool (a tool used in scrapbooking and other arts to press paper without damaging it). For this purpose, the burnishing tool will be used to score lines on paper tiles that will serve as a cutting guide.

Sunflower Trivet

Step 1

Cut an 8" square from ¼" hardboard and sand the edges. If you don't have access to a saw, you can use foam-core board for this project; but it will not hold up to use as well as hardboard.

Step 2

Prime and paint the trivet black.

Step 3

Draw a sunflower design in the center of the trivet in pencil.

Step 4

Prepare yellow, brown, and red papers, backing them with posterboard as learned in previous projects.

Step 5

Cut yellow and brown papers into random shapes.

Step 6

Glue down the yellow and brown tiles, using the sunflower design as a guide. Let dry completely. You may need to use the wallpaper knife to trim edges and tile that overlap the pencil boundary.

Step 7

Cut the red paper into 1"-square tiles, and glue the first tile in the lower-right corner.

ARTIST'S TIP:

In this project, cut the yellow tiles long and thin to resemble sunflower petals. Cut the brown tiles small and chunky to resemble the texture of the inner portion of a sunflower.

Step 8

Continue gluing 1" tiles around the perimeter of the project, leaving a ½₂" space between each tile. Glue down all the 1" tiles you can; but if the tile will not fit without trimming, leave the space alone for now. Let the glue dry completely before continuing.

Step 9

Place a 1"-square red tile up against the other 1" tiles, leaving a ½₂" space along the edges. Do not put down glue at this time. The red tile will overlap the sunflower design. Using the burnishing tool, score the tile, using the ridge created by the sunflower tiles lying underneath as a guide.

■ ARTIST'S TIP:

When paper gets wet with glue, the edges curl and the paper can shift. Try to use enough glue to cover the surface, but not enough to ooze over tiles when they are pressed into place. Also, beware of tiles lifting and shifting. Gently press them down until the glue dries enough to hold them in place.

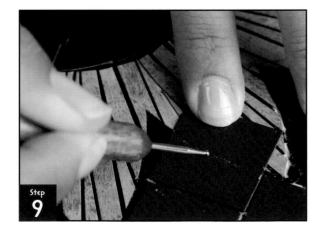

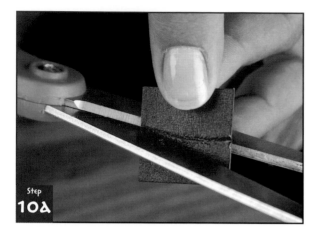

Step 10a

Step 10b

Step 13

Step 10

Trim the tile along the score line with scissors. Replace the tile and check the cut. Trim again if necessary. Include a ¹⁄₃₂" space between the red tile and sunflower.

Step 11

Repeat Step 9 on page 57 and step 10 for all remaining tiles until the entire background is filled in. Some tiles may be quite small and some cuts are tricky. Good luck, be patient, and don't worry—its only paper.

Step 12

Coat the surface with decoupage medium and let dry. Then spray polyurethane over the entire project and let dry.

Step 13

Cut a 7"-square piece from craft foam and glue it to the back of the trivet.

Backgammon Board   This backgammon board was completed using the same applications learned in Sunflower Trivet on pages 54-58. The triangles were laid out first, then the inner squares were fitted and trimmed using a burnishing tool. The border and edging are randomly placed squares and rectangles.

Technique 4
USING STAMPED IMAGES, PUNCHES, & SHAPED SCISSORS

One of the great things about paper mosaic is that you can use many of the new
paper tools that have become popular with scrapbooking and stamping.
Incorporating stamped tiles into your mosaics adds character and interest.
Embellishing these stamped images with punches and shaped scissors adds detail
and whimsy. Have fun with these tools; they add a dimension to the mosaic arts
that is truly unique to paper mosaic.

Refrigerator Magnets

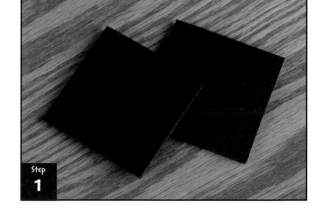

Step
1

Step 1
Cut a 2" square from black foam-core board.

Step 2
Cut a 1" square from a colorful piece
of paper.

ARTIST'S TIP:

I use all kinds of stamps in my paper mosaic designs, but have found that stamps with
little detail and nice shape are my favorites—particularly the inexpensive sponge stamps.
Mosaic is busy to begin with, and when I add stamps with a lot of detail, I might
take it too far. I prefer to stamp with paint rather than ink. Ink can smear when the
decoupage medium is applied. Those with more experience using ink may know of brands
that are more stable. Also, I like using paints for stamps because I can match the colors
I use to paint the mosaic papers.

Step 3

Brush paint on the surface of a stamp, then press the image onto the center of the 1" square and let dry.

Step 4

Cut strips of varying width (but not wider than ¾") from several different colored papers. Remember to prepare these papers by backing them with black posterboard.

Step 5

Glue the 1" square with the stamped image onto the black foam-core square.

Step 6

Using your creativity, randomly glue the strips to the edges around the center image, trimming as you go. Don't forget to leave a ½₂" space between the strips as you place them. When you're done, the surface should be covered with random chunks and slivers of small colored tile.

Step 7

Now comes the fun part. Using punches and shaped scissors, punch shapes and cute designs to embellish the magnet. Glue them into place and let the glue dry. Have fun—don't be shy!

Step 8

Brush the surface and edges with decoupage medium and let dry. You may have to decoupage this is two stages, brushing half the piece and letting it dry before brushing the other half.

Step 9

Seal the design with polyurethane. Once it has dried, glue a button magnet on the back.

Step 7a

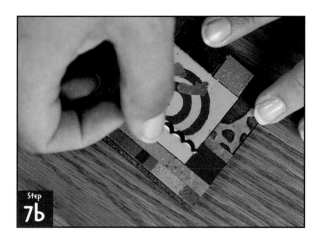

Step 7b

ARTIST'S TIP:

Color can be intimidating, but here's a way to gain experience and confidence working with color. Go to a fabric store and find a multicolored fabric you like. Take a piece home and paint it or find prepainted papers that match the fabric. Get the colors as close as possible, then proceed with your paper mosaic project. Chances are if you like the color combinations in the fabric, you will like them in your paper mosaic.

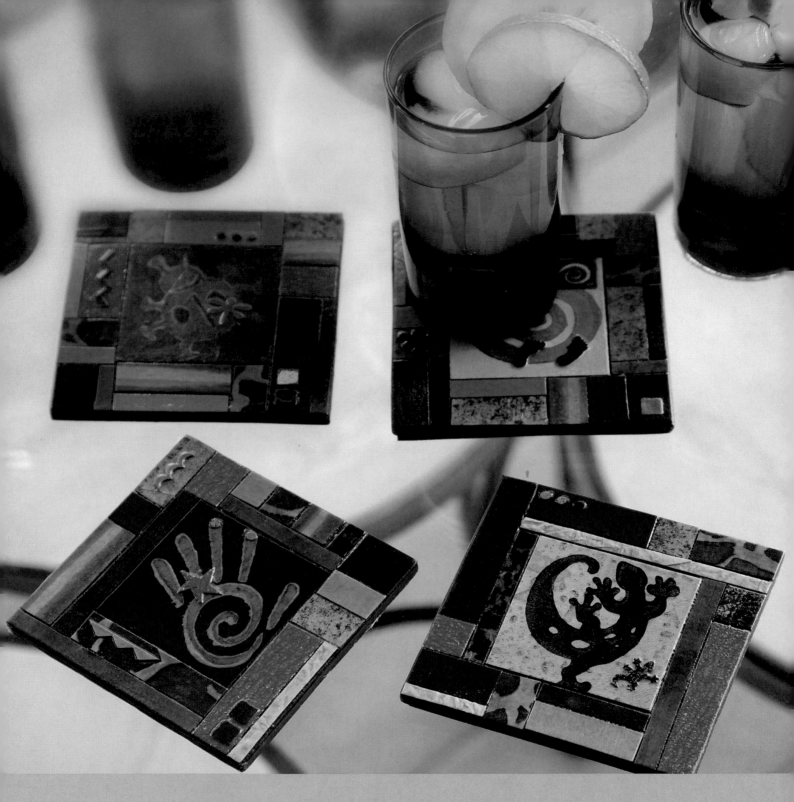

Coaster These coasters were designed in the same way as the Refrigerator Magnets in Technique 4 on pages 60–63. The base of the coaster is a 4" square constructed from ¼" hardboard. They are finished on the back with black craft foam. You may construct these coasters from foam-core board but may find they don't wear as well as hardboard. Also, I would suggest several coats of polyurethane for these coasters, as they will have prolonged exposure to moisture.

Picture Frame   Stamped images and a colorful collection of squares and rectangles transformed this simple craft frame into a whimsical piece of art. The craft frame was an inexpensive unfinished frame that I found at my local craft supply store. The only tricky part of this project is trimming tiles around the curved corners and fitting the inner and outer edges. When fitting inner and outer edges, trim the tiles approximately ⅛" thinner than the width of the edge.

Technique 5
LAYERING MOSAIC TILES

Once again, you are able to explore a technique that is unique to paper mosaic: the layering of paper tiles. You have a little bit of experience with layering paper from the Refrigerator magnets of Technique 4 on pages 63–65, layering punches and cut paper designs onto the tiles. However, in the next projects you will see how stacking several tiles creates a unique, modern look.

Step
2a

Stacked Square Box

Step 1

Cut the following shapes from black foam-core board: one 5¾" square, two 6⅜" squares, four 3" x 6" rectangles, and forty 1½" squares.

Step 2

Glue the box and lid together, using the photographs at right as a guide. Glue eight of the 1½" squares together to get a 1½" block. Repeat so that you have five 1½" blocks.

Step
2b

ARTIST'S TIP:

When doing stacked-mosaic projects, use a muffin tin to keep the different sized and colored papers organized.

Step
2c

Step 3

Paint four colors of paper or purchase colored, printed, or handmade papers. Glue them to black posterboard.

Step 4

Cut each piece of paper into the following shapes: twenty 1½" squares, twenty 1¼" squares, twenty 1" squares, and twenty ¾" squares.

Step 5

Glue a ¾" square onto a 1" square of a different color. Then glue this stacked tile onto a 1¼" square of a third color. Finally, glue this triple-stacked tile onto a 1½" square. All four squares should be different colors. Repeat this process until all the tiles are stacked, alternating the colors so that there is a variety of color combinations.

ARTIST'S TIP:

The thickness of stacked tiles tends to make them curl. Carefully glue the pieces together, pressing the edges until they catch. Then place the tiles under a piece of Plexiglas and place weights on top of the Plexiglas. This will help hold the edges down and keep the tile from curling too much.

Step 6

Glue the stacked tiles along the bottom edge of the box, leaving a ½" space between tiles. Four tiles should fit perfectly, so there is no need to trim them. Continue gluing all the tiles into place, alternating colors so that you have a nice color balance. Once the sides of the box are covered, glue tiles onto the lid.

Step 7

Glue tiles around four sides of four 1½" cubes and five sides of the remaining cube.

Step 8

Coat the box, the lid and the five cubes with decoupage medium and let dry.

Step 9

Glue the cubes that have tiles on four sides to the bottom corners of the box and the cube that has tiles on five sides to the center of the lid.

Step 10

Spray polyurethane over the entire piece and let dry.

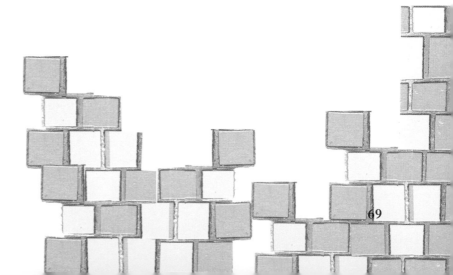

Stacked Tile Clock   This clock was made using the same basic application learned in Technique 5 on pages 80–86 with one difference: the tile edges were rounded off with a pair of scissors prior to gluing them together. The clock base was constructed from ¼" hardboard and 1" x 2" pine. Details of the construction for this style of clock are provided in the Dragonfly Clock on pages 80–86.

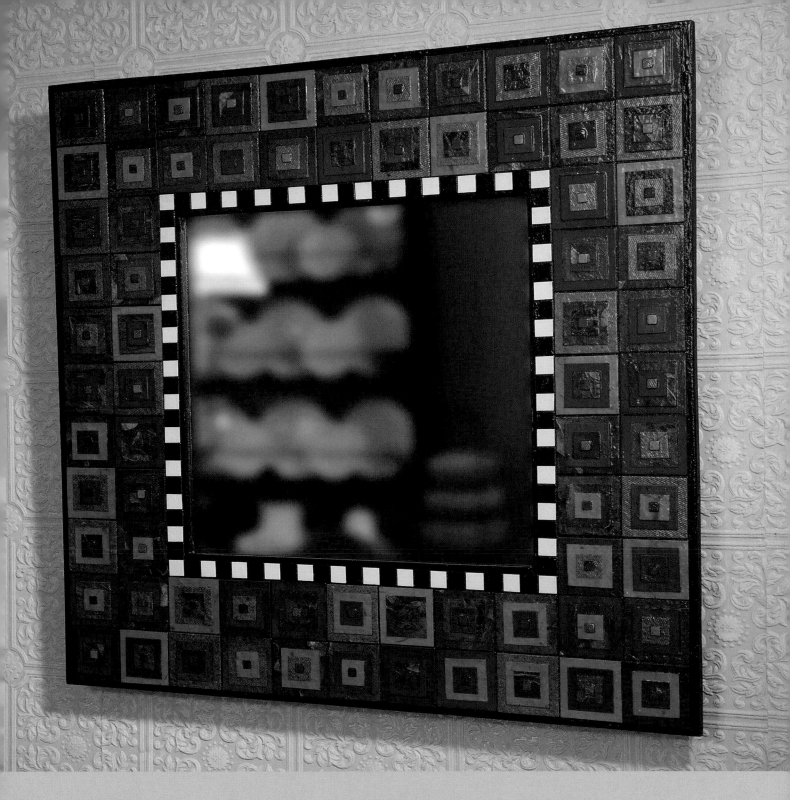

Stacked Tile Mirror   This mirror is very similar to the Stacked Square Box pages 66–69, but with an inner edge of ½" black-and-white tiles. The trickiest part of doing a project like this is to determine how many tiles will fit evenly on the surface of the frame. It is necessary that the tiles line up perfectly (both vertically and horizontally), so be careful in measuring the frame and factor in the space you want between tiles in order to determine the number and size of tiles you will need.

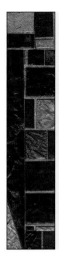

Technique 6
WORKING WITH TRANSPARENT BACKGROUNDS

This technique introduces a new material that will become the cornerstone of some of the more complicated paper mosaic projects—laminate film. Laminate film enables us to make mosaic projects with transparent grout lines. When light shines behind the mosaic, the grout lines illuminate, showing beautiful and unique geometric designs.

Night-light

Step 1

Cut a 3" x 4" rectangle from black foam-core board.

Step 2

Cut a 2" x 3" opening in the center of the foam-core rectangle, leaving a ¾" border.

Step 3

Cut a variety of squares, rectangles, and paper strips from colored papers thickened with posterboard.

Step 4

Using a paper punch, punch images in several of the squares and rectangles.

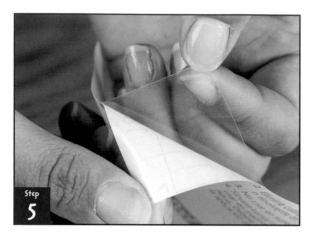

ARTIST'S TIP:

Color and layout are equally important in projects that have transparent backgrounds. In the daytime, when the light is off, only the colored tiles will show. At nighttime, when the light is on, the light between the tiles will show. Remember this when laying out the tiles and try to make the "grout lines" uniformly even.

Step 5

Cut a 2" x 3" piece from laminate film, and carefully peal off the backing. Place the film, sticky side up, on the work surface.

Step 6

Using the rectangles, squares, and strips of paper, layout an interesting design, leaving ½₂" between tiles.

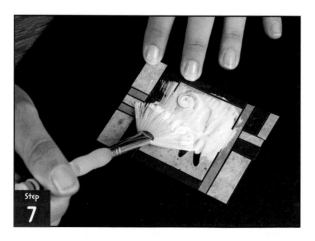

Step 7

Cover the laminate sheet with decoupage medium and let it dry.

Step 8

Brush decoupage medium on the frame and let it dry.

Step 9

Glue the laminate sheet behind the frame. There should be a ¼" overlap on all four sides of the laminate sheet. Let the glue dry.

Step 10

Spray polyurethane over the entire night-light.

Step 11

Glue a night-light mechanism to the back of the frame. Make sure the night-light leaves at least ¾" space between the bulb and the mosaic.

ARTIST'S TIP:

When working with transparent backgrounds, take full advantage of the wonderful paper punches available at scrapbooking stores. Also, many stores have diecut areas where you can use the stores die-cutting machine for a nominal fee.

Lampshade This lampshade uses the same technique used in the Night-light on pages 72–75, but on a much larger scale. This lampshade was constructed from laminate film, but you could achieve similar results with a store-bought lampshade made from a sheer material.

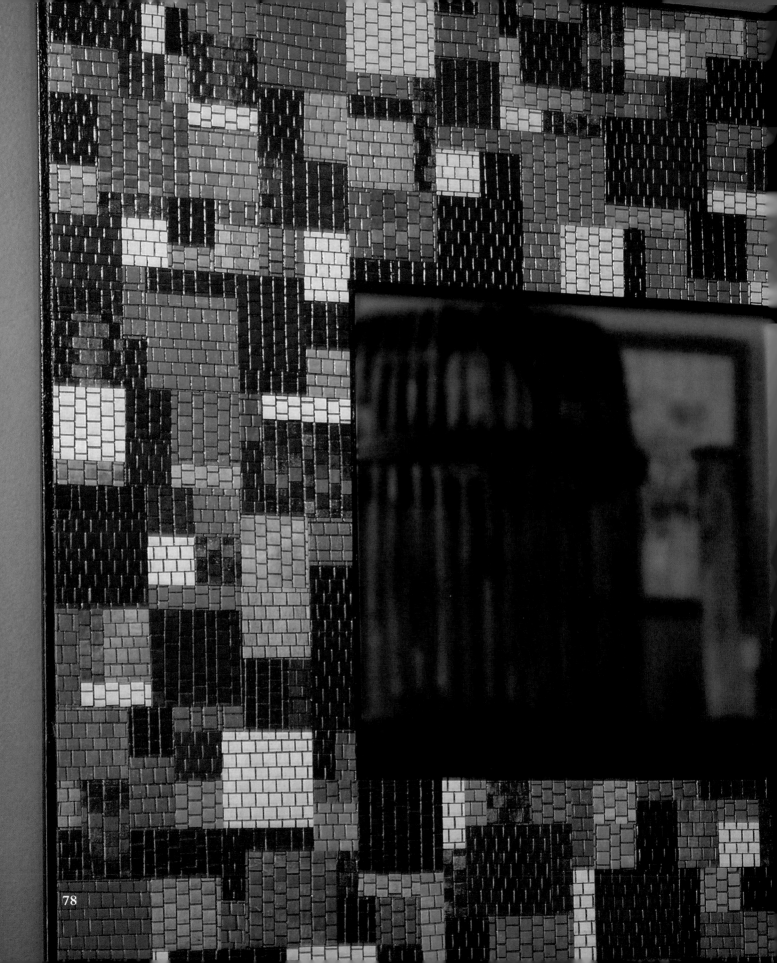

CREATING MOSAIC PATTERNS

B y using clear laminate film as a backing material, you can cut and place paper in order to make a composite sheet of tile. This composite sheet of tile can then be cut into a pattern and placed with other pattern pieces to create complex and intricate designs. Using patterns in paper mosaic is similar to using patterns in quilting or dressmaking: the design is broken into pattern pieces, then the pieces are assembled to create a harmonious design. In Technique 7, Dragonfly Clock on pages 80–86, you will learn how to translate mosaic design into patterns, how to create pattern pieces, and how to assemble a patterned mosaic.

Technique 7
CREATING MOSAIC SHEETS & USING PATTERNS

In the previous technique, laminate film introduced a transparent surface for creating paper mosaic projects. Now you will learn to use laminate film as a backing material that will enable you to create sheets of mosaic tile. Once you have sheets of mosaic tile, you can cut them into pattern pieces and glue them onto forms.

Dragonfly Clock

Step 1

Cut an 8" x 12" piece from ¼" hardboard for the clock face and sand the edges. If you do not have access to woodworking equipment, you may cut the face from black foam-core board.

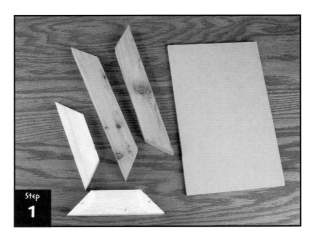

Step 2

Create a frame from 1" x 2" pine with the outer dimensions of 6" x 10". Use wood glue and staples to hold the mitered corners together. Sand the frame, then center it on the back side of the clock and glue it into place. After the glue has dried, prime and paint the clock black. You can construct this frame from foam-core board by cutting four frames with outer dimensions of 6" x 10" and inner dimensions of 4" x 8", then

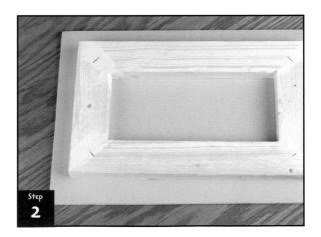

gluing them together in a stack. Center this stack on the back of the 8" x 12" foam-core board and glue it into place. This frame houses the clock mechanism.

Step 3

Cut a 8" x 12" piece from laminate film and place it on the work surface, paper side up.

Step 4

Sketch an image of a dragonfly onto the center of the laminate film (tracing on the paper side). Once you are happy with the design, go over the outer perimeter of the dragonfly with a black marker. The black outline should be uniformly ⅛" thick. Turn the sheet over and trace the black outline again on the laminate side of the film. The dragonfly outline should be clearly outlined on both the paper and laminate sides of the film.

Step 5

Carefully cut out the dragonfly. Cut in the center of the black outline, leaving ¹⁄₁₆" on the edges of the dragonfly and ¹⁄₁₆" on the background sheet. Place the dragonfly cutout and the cut-out background aside.

Step 6

Prepare two colors of paper for mosaic tiles by backing them with posterboard. Cut the paper used for the dragonfly into twenty-two ½" strips. Cut the paper used for the background into twelve 1" strips.

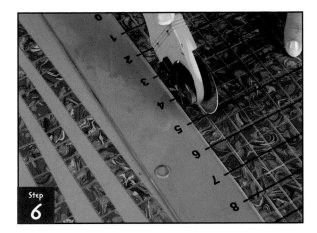

Step 7

Cut two 12" squares from laminate film. Carefully peel the backing off one piece of film and place it on the work surface, sticky side up. Press a ½" strip along the lower edge of the film, paper side up and posterboard side stuck to the film. Repeat with a second strip, leaving a ¹⁄₃₂" space between strips. Continue laying down strips until the entire film is covered. Repeat this process on the remaining piece of laminate film with the 1" strips.

Step 8

Place the sheet of ½" strips onto a cutting mat. Place the cutting grid on top of the sheet with the cutting slits running perpendicular to the strips of paper. Use a rotary cutter to cut the paper every ½". You should now have strips of ½" squares. Repeat this process for the sheet of 1" strips, but cut every 1" so that you have strips of 1" squares.

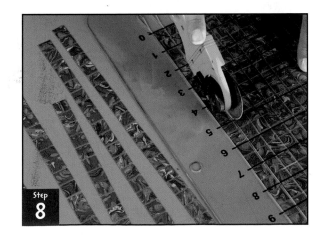

Step 9

Cut two more 12"-square sheets from laminate film. Peel the paper backing off of the film and place it sticky side up on the work surface. Carefully place a strip of ½" squares along the lower edge of the film. Repeat with a second strip, being careful to line up the space between the tiles with the row below. Place all the strips of tiles until the film is filled. Repeat this process with the strips of 1" tiles.

Step 10

Apply a thin coat of decoupage medium to both sheets of mosaic tile and let them dry.

Step 11

After the medium has dried, place both sheets of tile face down on the work surface. Gently peel the paper backing off the dragonfly image and stick the image onto the back of the sheet of ½" tiles. Peel the paper backing off the background sheet of laminate and stick it onto the back of the sheet of 1" tiles. Try to line up the edges of the background laminate with the center of the tiles so that you will not end up with little slivers of tiles when you trim this sheet.

Step 12

For the background laminate, trim the outer perimeter to 8" x 12" using the film edge as a guideline. The film edge is not as easy to see as the black marker edge, but if you hold it up to a light, you should be able to see it well enough. Carefully trim around the inner dragonfly image, using the marker line as a guide. Using either a wallpaper knife or scissors, trim the image so that there is no black outline remaining. You should be left with an 8" x 12" sheet of 1" squares with a dragonfly opening in the center.

Step 13

Trim the dragonfly image with a wallpaper knife or scissors, removing all of the black edge.

ARTIST'S TIP:

The paper used to make the mosaic dragonfly is a hand-marbled paper from Italy. I wanted to preserve the pattern in the paper, so I carefully cut and placed the papers so that the marbled pattern remained. If you look closely, you will see that the paint looks like it is flowing from one tile to the next.

Step 12a

Step 12b

Step 13

Step 14

Layout the two pieces onto a work surface. They should fit together perfectly with a ³⁄₁₆" space between the dragonfly and the background. Trim any areas that are necessary.

Step 15

Glue the two pieces onto the surface of the clock. After they have dried, apply a thin coat of decoupage medium to the surface and edges, and let it dry. Finally, spray the clock with polyurethane and let it dry.

Step 16

Install the clock mechanism according to the manufacturer's directions.

ARTIST'S TIP:

Working with pattern pieces can be tricky because as you cut the pattern, you may create tiny pieces of mosaic tile. If some of these pieces fall off of the laminate film, don't worry, just set them aside. Once all the pattern pieces are glued down, you can simply glue these small pieces into place.

Tulips Wall Hanging   I designed this piece using the same techniques learned in the Dragonfly Clock on pages 80–86. All of the tiles in this piece are uniformly small, only ¼" square. The papers used for this piece are an eclectic blend of papers that I hand-painted, hand-made banana bark papers from Thailand, and marbled papers from France.

"Life shrinks
or expands
in proportion
to one's
courage."

Anaïs Nin

SECTION 4

CREATING COMPLEX MOSAIC PAPERS

I n the previous section, you learned how to create mosaic patterns with the use of clear laminate film. In this section, you will build on this knowledge by creating complex sheets of mosaic tile, but with a different look. By varying the color, texture and size of the paper used, you can create interesting sheets of tile that can be used in a variety of projects. In this section, you will learn how to create whimsical and colorful sheets of tile to be used alone or paired with stamped images. You will also learn that with controlled cutting and placement techniques, you can create mosaics that look fresh, interesting, and quite unlike traditional mosaics.

Technique 8
CREATING MOSAIC SHEETS WITH RANDOM SIZED TILES

This technique is similar to Technique 7, the Dragonfly Clock on pages 80–86 because we place strips of paper onto laminate film to create composite sheets of mosaic tiles. The technique differs because we will be using a variety of colors and widths of paper to create a random and whimsical look.

Hanging Ornaments

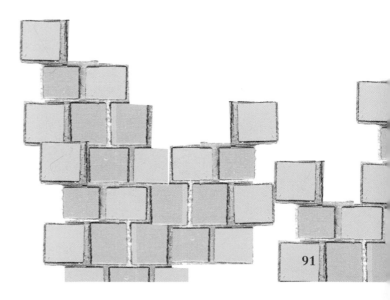

Step
1

Step 1

Lightly sand, prime, and paint a wooden ornament (available at craft stores).

Step 2

Prepare at least four different colors of papers by backing them with posterboard. You may also use paper left over from previous projects, but make sure you use complementary color tones.

Step 3

Cut the papers into strips of varying widths, from ⅛" up to ¾".

Step 4

Cut a 12"-square sheet from laminate film and remove the paper backing. Place the film on the work surface, sticky side up.

Step 5

Place a strip of paper along the lower edge of the film. Place a second strip of paper above the first, leaving a ½₂" space between strips. Continue placing strips of paper (varying the width and color) until the film is covered.

Step 6

Place the sheet of paper strips, film side down, on a cutting mat. Position a straightedge perpendicular to the paper strips and use a rotary cutter to cut varying widths of strips.

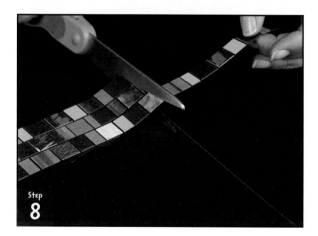

Step 7

Cut another 12"-square piece from laminate film and peel off the paper backing. Place the film on the work surface, sticky side up, and place a strip of squares and rectangles along the bottom edge.

ARTIST'S TIP:

When I cut varying widths of papers, I find that using a straightedge and rotary cutter is less cumbersome than the cutting grid. However, please be particularly careful when cutting with a straightedge, as there is less control than with a cutting grid.

Step 8

As you place the strips of tile, vary the placement so that you have movement of shape and color. Every third or fourth strip, place a strip far to the right side of the laminate sheet so that a portion hangs off the edge. Then cut off the portion hanging over the edge and place it to the left. This keeps colors and shapes shifting from row to row, so that you don't get a clumping of color.

Continue placing all the strips until the sheet is full.

Step 9

Brush a thin coat of decoupage medium onto the sheet of mosaic tiles and let it dry.

Step 10

Place the sheet of tiles on the work surface, face down. Place the ornament on the back of the tiles and trace around its perimeter with a marker.

Step 11

Cut the sheet of paper tiles along the inside edge of the marker line. There should be no marker line left on the tile cutout.

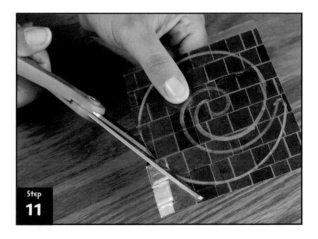

Step 12

Glue the tile cutout onto the wooden ornament and let dry.

Step 13

Decoupage the entire ornament and let dry. Spray polyurethane on the ornament and let dry.

Step 14

Drill a small hole in the ornament and place gold thread through the ornament for hanging.

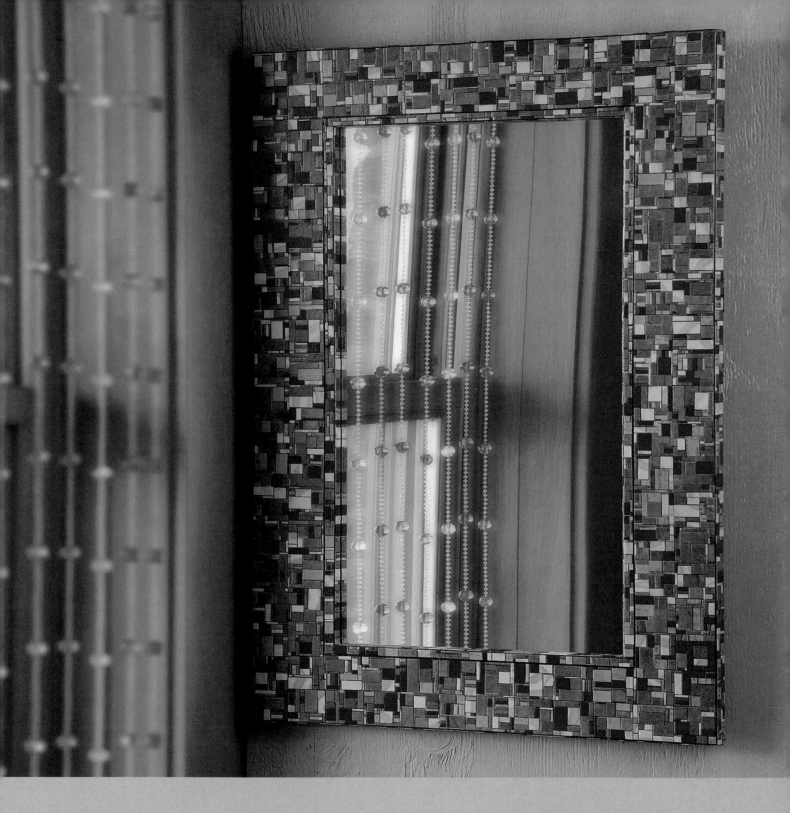

Primary Color Mirror   The paper tiles used in this mirror were created using the same techniques learned in the Hanging Ornaments project on pages 90–93. However, once the sheets of mosaic tiles were completed, I cut them into 1" squares, then glued the squares onto the frame.

Mirror in Color Transition   In this piece, I created sheets of mosaic tiles, cut the sheets into 1" squares, and glued them onto the form. However, the style of this piece is unique because I consciously controlled the placement of color so that the colors look like they are transitioning from one to another.

Technique 9
COMBINING MOSAIC SHEETS, LAYERING & STAMPED IMAGES

This technique is really a combination of three previously learned techniques, but deserves its own headline because the results are so wonderful. Over the years of making paper mosaics and selling them to the public, I have found that projects done using this technique get the most attention. Perhaps people connect with the whimsical look of this design.

Door Hanger

Step 1

Cut a piece of foam-core board, using the illustration at right as a guide.

Step 2

Prepare a sheet of mosaic tiles, using the technique learned in Technique 8, pages 93–95, Steps 2–8.

Step 3

Cut the following shapes of posterboard-backed paper: one 3" square, two 3" x 3½" rectangles.

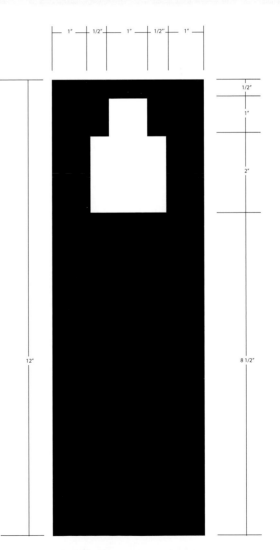

Step 4

Cut one 3" x 3½" square as shown in the illustration at right.

Step 5

Cut strips from the sheet of mosaic tile in the following dimensions: two ½" x 12" strips, four ½" x 3" strips.

Step 6

Layout the squares of papers and strips of tiles as shown in the photograph below, and glue to the foam-core form.

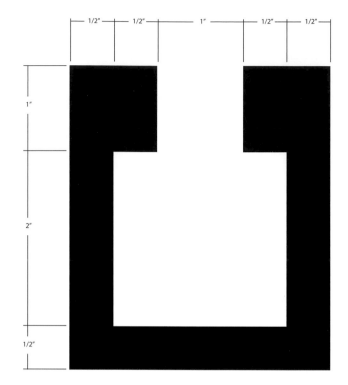

Step 6

ARTIST'S TIP:

Before backing the paper with posterboard, you can add words or inspirational quotes by running it through a printer. Typeset the words and quotes to fit within an appropriate sized box for whatever project you are working on.

Step 7

Glue a 2"-square tile onto the lower section. Embellish the lower square with stamped images and punches. Write a message on a 2" x 3" rectangle of complementary paper and glue it onto the center square.

Step 7

Step 8

Brush decoupage medium over the entire project and let it dry. Spray it with polyurethane and let it dry.

ARTIST'S TIP:

You may find that you have more strips of paper than you know what to do with. To keep them organized, place them into potato chip cans—after you have eaten the chips and cleaned the cans, of course. The thin tall cans keep the strips from getting bent and help you keep the paper organized by color or project.

Hook Plate This hook plate is made from a 1" x 4" piece of pine and was designed using the same techniques learned in the Door Hanger project on pages 96–99. The edges were covered in a strip of mosaic sheet cut ⅛" thinner than the thickness of the board. For a piece like this that will have a lot of use, consider adding a second coat of decoupage medium around the corners and edges.

Whimsical Clock When designing , I always think about color and personality. If I am working with earth tones, I incorporate leaf and botanical images. If I am working with a palette that appeals to children, I use swirls, footprints, and silly things like ants holding balloons and frogs singing and dancing. If I'm using color in a variety of tones, I use whatever images feel right. I have found after years of doing this work that each piece has a personality and that if I pay attention, the piece "speaks to me" and I know exactly what images and embellishments to use.

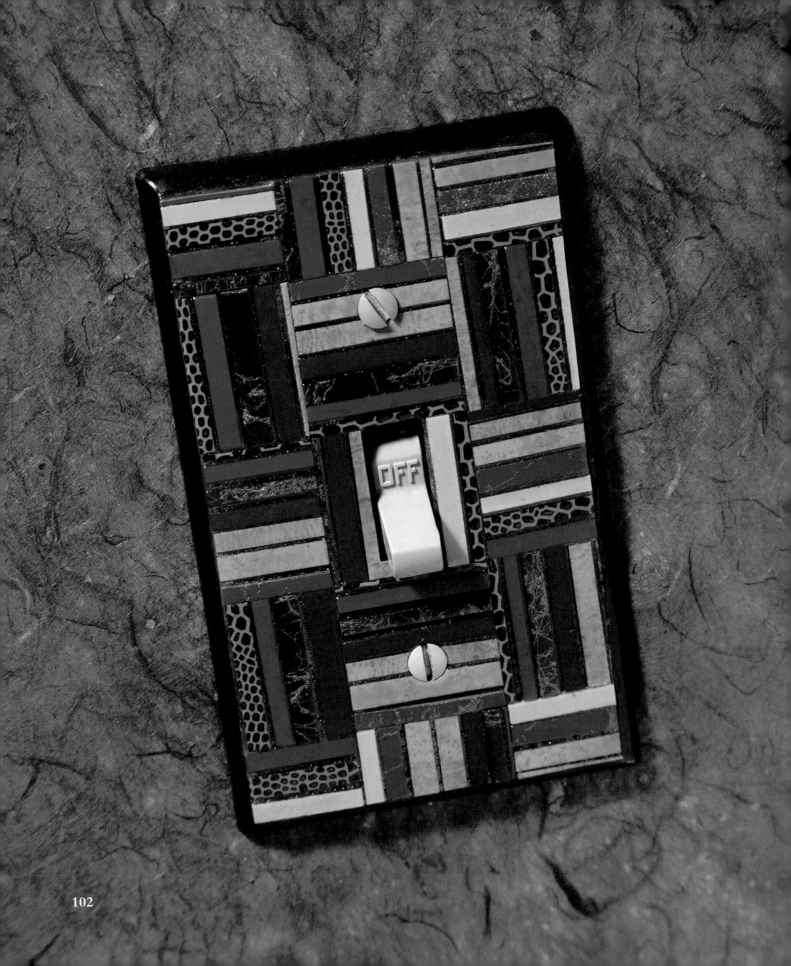

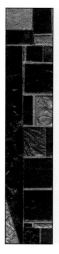

Technique 10
STRIP WEAVE

This final technique will show you how to create beautiful mosaics that look like a basket weave. Cutting paper strips into unique shapes is only limited by your imagination and in time you may find yourself developing new and unique cutting applications. The idea for this technique came to me one day when I was looking at a basket and found myself thinking, "What if...?"

Weave Switch Plate Cover

Step 1

Purchase a black or dark brown switch plate from a home improvement store.

Step 2

Measure the flat area of the switch plate (don't include the curved corners) and cut a template to those dimensions from posterboard.

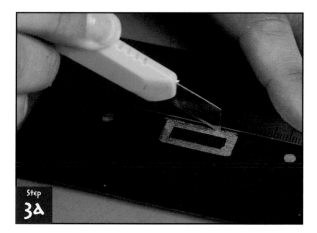

Step 3a

Step 3

Center the switch plate (face down) over the posterboard. Trace the inner edges of the holes and rectangular opening onto the posterboard with a marker. Use the marked lines as a guide to cut out the rectangular opening with a wallpaper knife. Use a hole punch to punch out the small circles.

Step 3b

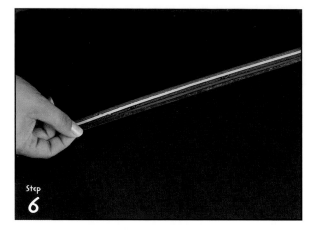

Step 4

Cut thin strips (approximately ⅛") from a variety of different-colored prepared papers.

Step 5

Cut a 12"-square sheet from laminate film. Carefully peel the paper backing off and place the laminate on the work surface, sticky side up.

Step 6

Carefully place the first strip of paper along the lower edge of the laminate. Repeat with additional strips until the sheet if full. Don't forget to leave a ½2" space between strips.

Step 7

Cover the entire sheet in a thin coat of decoupage medium and let it dry.

Step 8

Place the sheet of strips onto a cutting mat and place the cutting grid on top, with the cutting slits running perpendicular to the strips of paper. Using a rotary cutter, cut the sheet into 1" strips.

Step 9

Place a single strip under the cutting grid with the cutting slits running parallel to the paper strips. Cut the strip into 1" squares.

Step 10

Cut a piece from laminate film 1" wider and longer than the switch-plate template and place it paper side up on the work surface. Center the switch-plate template on the sheet. Use a marker to trace around the template and inside the rectangle and small holes.

Step 10

Step 11

Carefully remove the paper backing and place it sticky side up on the work surface.

■ ARTIST'S TIP:

When covered in decoupage medium, thin strips of paper tend to lift, curl, and buckle more than thicker strips. To minimize this problem, tape the edges of the sheet of strips to a piece of Plexiglas prior to applying the decoupage medium. After the medium dries, place another piece of Plexiglas on top and place something heavy on it. This will push most of the strips back into place.

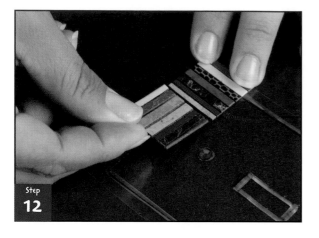

Step 12

Starting at the lower-right corner, place a tile with the strips going up and down. Next to it, place a tile with the strips going side to side. I leave almost no space between weave tiles as I place them, but you may prefer how it looks with a little space.

Step 13

Continue placing tiles until the laminate sheet is full, alternating the placement of the tiles so that it resembles a basket weave.

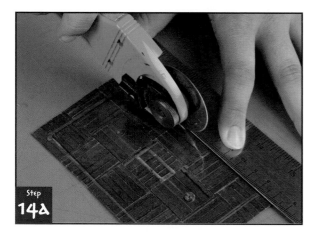

Step 14

Trim the perimeter of the weave tiles with a rotary cutter and straightedge. Use a wallpaper knife to trim the small rectangle in the center. Use a hole punch to punch out the circles.

Step 15

Step 15

Glue the sheet of weave tiles onto the switch plate, making sure the rectangle and holes are lined up properly. Press out any bubbles and let the glue dry.

Step 16

Brush decoupage medium onto the surface and edges of the switch plate and let dry. Spray with a coat of polyurethane and let dry.

Step 16

ARTIST'S TIP:

Weaves are great projects to use up miscellaneous papers. Even small amounts of paper can be cut into thin strips and incorporated into the design. The more color, the merrier, in these weaves. However, don't forget to keep the majority of the colors either warm or cool. Too much mixing can make a project look muddy.

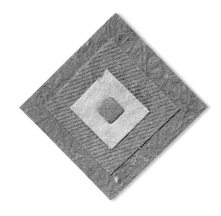

Weave Mirror   This weave mirror was designed using almost the same techniques as in the Weave Switchplate on pages 102–107. However, rather than applying the tiles onto a laminate sheet, they were glued directly onto the mirror frame. When making a project like this, be careful with placement—a row of tiles rarely fits perfectly on the frame. Sometimes you have to trim tiles; sometimes you have to add a strip of paper to make a tile wider. The main thing to remember is to keep the tiles in line and to alternate the direction of the paper strips with each tile.

Aztec Clock   I designed this clock using a similar technique to that used in the weave mirrors. However, for the edge, I cut the strips on an angle, then reassembled them into a chevron pattern. The center sections are simply thin strips of tile that I carefully trim to fit.

CHAPTER THREE
Gallery

"Time is a Woman's Best Friend" Art Clock   This piece is a patterned mosaic that is made completely from rice papers. It uses all the different design styles learned in this book to create a unique look for each of the pattern pieces. Some sections have uniform sized ½" square tiles, other sections have thin strips arranged in a weave pattern, and still other sections have randomly sized chunks and slivers.

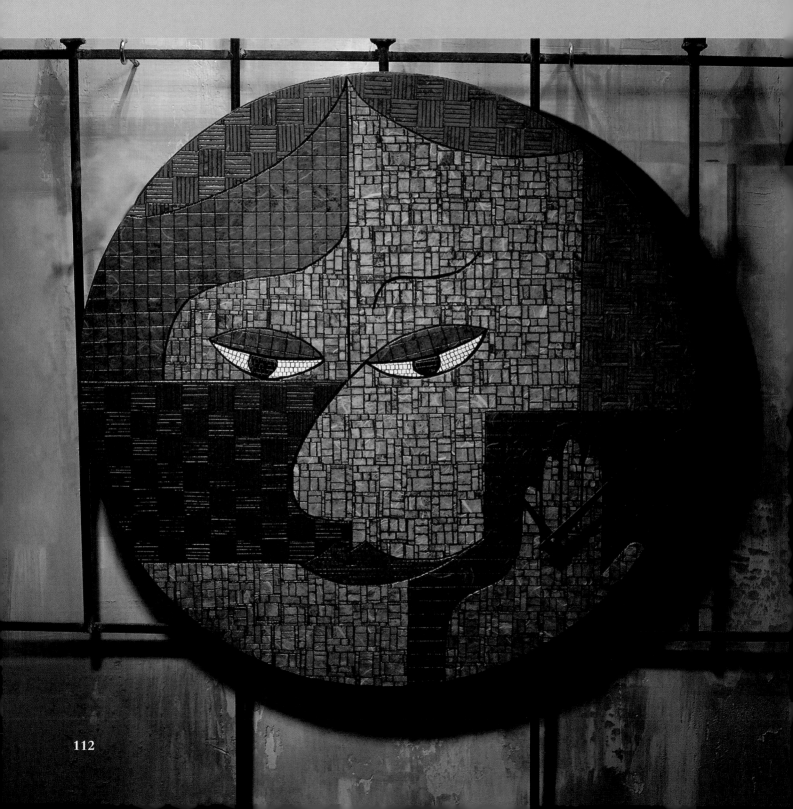

"Embrace" Wall Hanging   This wall hanging is made completely from hand-painted papers that were painted with a brayer (a printmaker's inking tool that looks like a small, rubber rolling pin). Painting papers with a brayer will mottle the paints and give them an interesting texture. The couple shown in the design were constructed from pattern pieces, while the background was filled in with a random placement of geometric elements.

Table in Earth Tones This table is made with a border of large stamped and embellished tiles with strips of mosaic tile laid between these tiles and on the edge. The center section is 1½" square tiles made from a coffee-stained piece of paper. Really! It wasn't an accident, I just happened to be pondering what color to paint a piece of white paper when my eyes fell on some cold coffee left over from breakfast.

Kitchen Table This table was one of my first large paper-mosaic projects, and it is still one of my favorites. I did not use punches or shaped scissors in this piece, but the stamped images are obvious. The surface was coated with decoupage medium as usual, but received five coats of polyurethane, which I applied with a roller. After years of constant use, it looks the same as it did the week I made it.

115

Patchwork Table and Mirror Set This table and mirror set was designed in a patchwork style and integrates squares of paper and squares of composite tile. The papers used in this set include handmade chiri bark, embossed handmade paper, embossed reptile-patterned paper, straw mat, and cork.

Mosaic "Sundance" Mirror This mirror was constructed from ¾" plywood with a scroll saw. Several of the edges of the mirror were cut at a 90 degree angle so that the mosaic edging would show more dramatically. The tiles were cut from composite sheets of tile, and the placement was controlled to make the colors change from center to outer edge.

Matchstick Mirror The technique for creating this mirror is unique because all of the tiles are cut very thin and long to resemble matchsticks. This weave technique is similar to the Weave Switchplate on pages 102–107, but the width and color of the strips is varied to create lively movement.

Children's Growth Stick This wall hanging is designed to chart your children's growth as well as to remind us of all the things we need to do every day: to be kind, to dream big, to believe in yourself, and to enjoy your cookies! The piece is created from stamped and painted images interspersed with strips of composite tile.

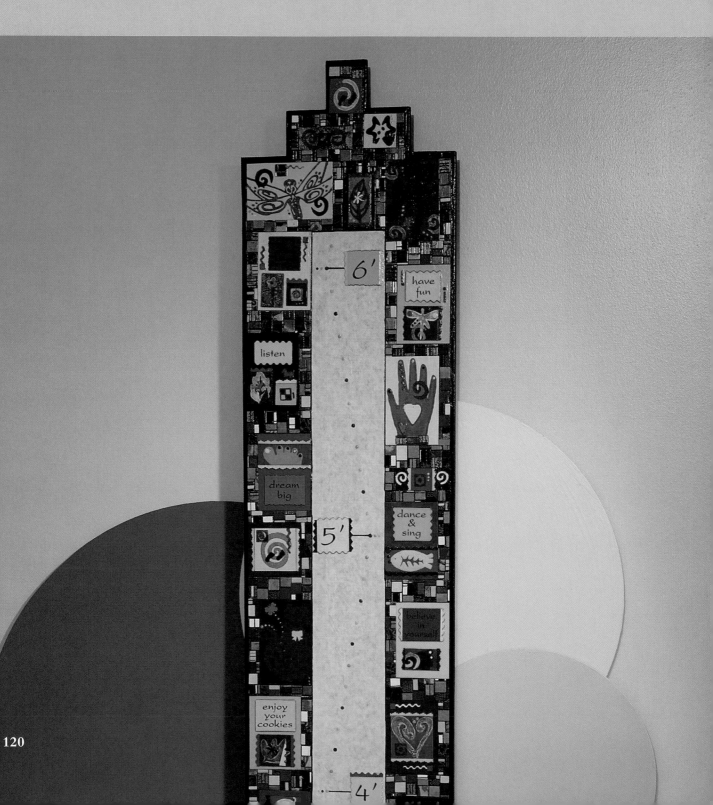

Geometric Mirror in Jewel Tones This mirror is a whimsical compilation of triangles, squares, and strips of composite tile. In creating this and other pieces like it, I work strictly from intuition with no pattern in mind. I start gluing down elements and work my way around the mirror until it is finished.

Geometric Mirror in Red Tones This geometric mirror is similar to the geometric mirror in jewel tones on page 121 but has some stamping and painting embellishments. When creating a piece like this, I always think about color, balance, and flow. A piece has balance when color and texture do not dominate a certain section. A piece has nice flow when the elements are arranged in a manner pleasing to the eye.

122

Peacock Tabletop This peacock is made from hand-painted papers and tissue papers. The teal feathers are a combination of three papers: teal tissue paper, a hand-painted paper, and a marbled paper from Italy. The body is made from gold tissue paper and the black elements are made from hand-painted paper. The twelve feathers, body, and surrounding areas are all individual pattern pieces that were pieced together on ¾″ plywood.

INDEX

INDEX

ABOUT THE AUTHOR

Susan Seymour has a broad background in Adult Education and Research, but no formal training in art. She made her first mosaic project from broken tile and was hooked, completing several projects before moving on to explore paper arts. For more than a year she experimented with paper painting, collage, and papermaking before combining these with her love of mosaic.

She is now a full-time professional artist exhibiting and selling her artwork at festivals across the southwest region of the United States. She lives near Park City, Utah, with her husband and two children.

For more of Susan's work visit her website **www.papermosaic.net**

Metric Equivalency Chart

mm-millimeters   cm-centimeters
inches to millimeters and centimeters

inches	mm	cm	inches	cm	inches	cm
$\frac{1}{8}$	3	0.3	9	22.9	30	76.2
$\frac{1}{4}$	6	0.6	10	25.4	31	78.7
$\frac{1}{2}$	13	1.3	12	30.5	33	83.8
$\frac{5}{8}$	16	1.6	13	33.0	34	86.4
$\frac{3}{4}$	19	1.9	14	35.6	35	88.9
$\frac{7}{8}$	22	2.2	15	38.1	36	91.4
1	25	2.5	16	40.6	37	94.0
$1\frac{1}{4}$	32	3.2	17	43.2	38	96.5
$1\frac{1}{2}$	38	3.8	18	45.7	39	99.1
$1\frac{3}{4}$	44	4.4	19	48.3	40	101.6
2	51	5.1	20	50.8	41	104.1
$2\frac{1}{2}$	64	6.4	21	53.3	42	106.7
3	76	7.6	22	55.9	43	109.2
$3\frac{1}{2}$	89	8.9	23	58.4	44	111.8
4	102	10.2	24	61.0	45	114.3
$4\frac{1}{2}$	114	11.4	25	63.5	46	116.8
5	127	12.7	26	66.0	47	119.4
6	152	15.2	27	68.6	48	121.9
7	178	17.8	28	71.1	49	124.5
8	203	20.3	29	73.7	50	127.0

yards to meters

yards	meters	yards	meters	yards	meters	yards	meters	yards	meters
$\frac{1}{8}$	0.11	$2\frac{1}{8}$	1.94	$4\frac{1}{8}$	3.77	$6\frac{1}{8}$	5.60	$8\frac{1}{8}$	7.43
$\frac{1}{4}$	0.23	$2\frac{1}{4}$	2.06	$4\frac{1}{4}$	3.89	$6\frac{1}{4}$	5.72	$8\frac{1}{4}$	7.54
$\frac{3}{8}$	0.34	$2\frac{3}{8}$	2.17	$4\frac{3}{8}$	4.00	$6\frac{3}{8}$	5.83	$8\frac{3}{8}$	7.66
$\frac{1}{2}$	0.46	$2\frac{1}{2}$	2.29	$4\frac{1}{2}$	4.11	$6\frac{1}{2}$	5.94	$8\frac{1}{2}$	7.77
$\frac{5}{8}$	0.57	$2\frac{5}{8}$	2.40	$4\frac{5}{8}$	4.23	$6\frac{5}{8}$	6.06	$8\frac{5}{8}$	7.89
$\frac{3}{4}$	0.69	$2\frac{3}{4}$	2.51	$4\frac{3}{4}$	4.34	$6\frac{3}{4}$	6.17	$8\frac{3}{4}$	8.00
$\frac{7}{8}$	0.80	$2\frac{7}{8}$	2.63	$4\frac{7}{8}$	4.46	$6\frac{7}{8}$	6.29	$8\frac{7}{8}$	8.12
1	0.91	3	2.74	5	4.57	7	6.40	9	8.23
$1\frac{1}{8}$	1.03	$3\frac{1}{8}$	2.86	$5\frac{1}{8}$	4.69	$7\frac{1}{8}$	6.52	$9\frac{1}{8}$	8.34
$1\frac{1}{4}$	1.14	$3\frac{1}{4}$	2.97	$5\frac{1}{4}$	4.80	$7\frac{1}{4}$	6.63	$9\frac{1}{4}$	8.46
$1\frac{3}{8}$	1.26	$3\frac{3}{8}$	3.09	$5\frac{3}{8}$	4.91	$7\frac{3}{8}$	6.74	$9\frac{3}{8}$	8.57
$1\frac{1}{2}$	1.37	$3\frac{1}{2}$	3.20	$5\frac{1}{2}$	5.03	$7\frac{1}{2}$	6.86	$9\frac{1}{2}$	8.69
$1\frac{5}{8}$	1.49	$3\frac{5}{8}$	3.31	$5\frac{5}{8}$	5.14	$7\frac{5}{8}$	6.97	$9\frac{5}{8}$	8.80
$1\frac{3}{4}$	1.60	$3\frac{3}{4}$	3.43	$5\frac{3}{4}$	5.26	$7\frac{3}{4}$	7.09	$9\frac{3}{4}$	8.92
$1\frac{7}{8}$	1.71	$3\frac{7}{8}$	3.54	$5\frac{7}{8}$	5.37	$7\frac{7}{8}$	7.20	$9\frac{7}{8}$	9.03
2	1.83	4	3.66	6	5.49	8	7.32	10	9.14